SINISTER SURFERS

In Antarctic waters off the coast of Patagonia, the killer whale practices a very sinister kind of surfing. It waits for a really big wave and rides it to shore—straight into a group of unsuspecting sea-lion pups. The hunter snaps a squealing pup in its mouth, just in time for the next wave to carry it back out to sea. Split-second timing saves the whale from being beached.

PLAYING WITH DINNER

Death is not instant for the baby sea lion. First the killer whale plays "catch," tossing its victim into the air and batting it with its tail. But before long, hunger takes over: the whale gulps down its prey in a single swallow.

BRAIN BONUS

How many types of whales and dolphins do killer whales attack?
a) 10
b) 15
c) 25

How fast can a killer whale swim?

a) 16 mph
b) 35 mph
c) 47 mph

How many teeth does a long-snouted spinner dolphin have?

a) up to 92
b) 93–171
c) 172–252

(answers on page 32)

BREATHING APPARATUS

Killer whales and dolphins are air-breathing mammals like us. They come to the surface to breathe every four to five minutes.

KILLING MACHINE

Once a shark knows you're there, you're in trouble! Hidden inside the shark's huge skull are two inner ears. The shark can hear the splashing of a likely victim from about half a mile away.

BUILT TO BEND

Instead of bones, sharks have skeletons made of cartilage. That's the same bendable stuff that you have in your ears and nose. This makes the shark's spine super-flexible and allows it to twist and turn in the water as it chases its prey.

GREEDY GUTS

Tiger sharks will gulp down almost anything. Items found inside their stomachs include a goat, ships' anchors, car license plates, whole suits of armor, tires, and, sometimes, human bodies!

Dorsal fin *This is the scary back fin that tells a swimmer that danger is coming! The shark uses this fin to keep its body balanced and level in the water.*

Tail fin *This fin gives the shark its great speed. By swishing its tail from side to side, the shark propels itself through the water.*

Blue Shark

BRAIN BONUS

Which of these fish is not a shark?

a) a whale shark
b) a dogfish
c) a megamouth

How long does an adult shark's set of teeth last?

a) about a week
b) a month or two
c) about a year

How many times faster than an Olympic swimmer can a tiger shark swim?

a) twice
b) three times
c) six times

(answers on page 32)

Pectoral fins

The flow of water over these front fins gives the shark lift in the water, like a plane's wings. Pectoral fins also help the shark to steer its course.

COLD-BLOODED KILLERS

Most sharks are cold-blooded, so their bodies stay at the same temperature as the water around them. Not so with the speed champions, such as the mako or the great white. These sharks keep their blood temperature higher than the surrounding water, which means their muscles are warm, too. Warm muscles can work harder: the great white has double the power of a cold-blooded shark.

TOOTHSOME TALES

Most sharks go through hundreds of pairs of teeth in a lifetime. The mako's teeth are especially terrifying. They look like rows of long daggers that can hold prey in a death grip.

Mako shark's teeth

5

SHARK ATTACK

The most feared ocean creature is probably the shark. This fierce predator is specifically designed for the hunt. The most powerful shark is the great white. Sleek and streamlined, it can shoot through the water at speeds of up to 20 mph.

Great white shark

SNIFFING OUT A MEAL

When finding a meal, the shark first hears its likely victim (usually a wounded animal) struggling. As it swims toward its target, the shark moves its head from side to side to pick up the scent. A shark can smell its victim's blood a quarter of a mile away.

FANG MONSTER

The prehistoric megalodon shark had teeth that were 6 inches long—that's a fangy four times longer than the great white's.

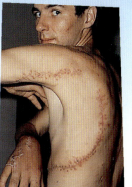

CLEAN CUT

The shark's teeth are so sharp that survivors of attacks say they didn't even feel the bite. Unfortunately, few of those attacked live to tell the tale. This fisherman was lucky—but the toothy scars from the hungry great white that attacked him are permanent.

A SPECIAL SENSE

Just before the shark bites, pores on its snout pick up tiny electrical signals from its victim's heart and muscles. Thanks to these super-sensitive pores, called ampullae of Lorenzini, the shark can pinpoint its prey's exact location, then snap shut its enormous jaws with amazing accuracy.

MAN-EATERS?

There are about 350 different species of shark, but most feed on large fish and seals—not human beings! Most of the sharks that have attacked humans were either provoked or simply made a mistake.

SINISTER SNAPPERS

Snappers school together and prowl the coral reefs, preying on small fish, crabs, and other crustaceans. Where did they get the name *snapper*? From the snapping of their dagger-toothed jaws!

School of snappers

BRAIN BONUS

How long is a bluefish?

a) 4 feet
b) 6.5 feet
c) 16 feet

Which of these is another name for bluefish?

a) shoaler
b) tailor
c) grouper

How many dorsal fins do barracuda and bluefish have?

a) one
b) two
c) three

(answers on page 32)

PREDATOR ALERT!

All barracuda are predators, but most feed on small fish such as anchovies or mullets. These fearless fish are well known for their curiosity and, of course, for their huge, sharp teeth. The great barracuda has occasionally been known to attack humans swimming in warm, tropical seas.

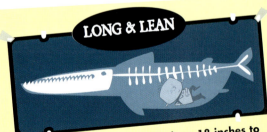

LONG & LEAN

Barracuda can be anywhere from 18 inches to over 6 feet long. The great barracuda is as long as an adult human is tall.

KILLER GANGS

When fierce hunters join forces to form monster gangs, the results can be devastating. Barracuda and bluefish are the piranhas of the seas, with teeth to match. They can wipe out a school of fish in minutes.

FEEDING FRENZY

Bluefish hunt in packs that are thousands strong. Together these killers work themselves up into a feeding frenzy, attacking anything in their way as they cruise through the water. They only have time to snap at their food, leaving behind a trail of blood and lots of half-eaten, dying fish.

Great barracuda

WHERE IN THE WORLD?

Bluefish and barracuda don't like to limit themselves to one region. They can be found in warm water all over the world.

HARMLESS GIANTS

Not all of the monsters of the deep are vicious predators! Some of the biggest, scariest-looking fish and sea mammals are completely harmless.

Unless you happen to be microscopic plankton or krill, that is!

WHAT A WHOPPER!

The whale shark may be the world's biggest fish, but it shares the oceans with an even bigger creature—the blue whale. Measuring 79 feet long and weighing 85 tons, this record-breaking mammal is the biggest creature on the planet.

Whale shark

SHIP TIPPER

Cruising whale sharks like to take it slow, and that's why they can spell trouble for us humans: sometimes boats have capsized after colliding with them. The collisions hurt the sharks, too. One whale shark had a fin taken off by a propeller.

How long is a whale shark?

a) 16 feet
b) 33 feet
c) 59 feet

What's the record for the longest blue whale?

a) 89 feet
b) 98 feet
c) 110 feet

Which shark also eats plankton and krill?

a) basking shark
b) great white
c) cookie cutter shark

(answers on page 32)

GENTLE GIANT

The whale shark may be enormous, but it is happy to feed on the smallest food in the sea—microscopic plants and animals called plankton or krill. Although it has thousands of tiny teeth, the whale shark doesn't bite or chew. Gill rakers—spongy mesh hanging in the shark's throat—sift the tiny food from water passing through the shark's mouth.

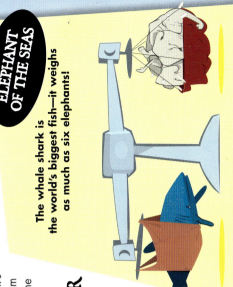

ELEPHANT OF THE SEAS

The whale shark is the world's biggest fish—it weighs as much as six elephants!

Whale shark

COLANDER MOUTH

Like the whale shark, the blue whale feeds on krill. In a single gulp, the whale takes in about 1,500 gallons of water. In one hour, that adds up to enough water to fill a swimming pool. The giant whale doesn't have any teeth. Special plates in its mouth made of a substance called baleen act as a sieve to filter out the tiny fish.

II

SLIPPERY SERPENTS

Snakes are scary enough on land, but did you know there are snakes in the sea, too? There are over 50 different species of sea snake, all found in tropical waters off the coasts of Australia and Asia, where the temperature is high enough to warm their cold-blooded bodies.

WRITHING WRIGGLERS

Most sea snakes live on coral reefs or in coastal mangrove swamps. Sometimes they join together to form a huge, wriggling mass. This writhing raft floats on the surface, basking in the warm rays of the sun.

Olive sea snake

SERPENT'S KISS

Like many land snakes, all sea snakes have a venomous bite. Luckily, sea snakes bite for only two reasons: either in self-defense or because they want to paralyze their prey (which includes creatures such as eels and fish). Like cobras, sea snakes inject their victims through their two fangs. Even the king cobra is no match for the Belcher's sea snake—its venom is 100 times more powerful than any other snake's.

The oarfish is the longest fish in the sea—as far as we know! It's as long as four canoes placed end to end.

THAT'S OAR-FULLY LONG!

FREAKY FISH

The most likely candidate to be a sea serpent is not a snake at all. The handsome oarfish usually lives in deep tropical waters, so few get to admire its long, silvery body and majestic red crest. Oarfish grow to a length of 30 feet, but in 1963, scientists spotted one swimming off New Jersey that was a whopping 50 feet long!

New Caledonian sea snake

DOING THE CONGA

The biggest-ever sea-snake party happened in 1932 in the Strait of Malacca, off Malaysia. Millions of *Astrotia stokesii,* or Stokes's sea snakes, formed a line that was 10 feet wide and 62 miles long!

BRAIN BONUS

Which other reptile lives in the ocean?

a) saltwater crocodile
b) garter snake
c) iguana

From which part of its body does a sea snake get rid of excess salt?

a) its bottom
b) its tongue
c) its ears

Which creature do the Japanese call "king of the palace under the sea"?

a) olive sea snake
b) great white shark
c) oarfish

(answers on page 32)

13

BIG SOFTIES

Who'd hang out with a predator? Strangely, lots of little creatures do seem to form friendships with underwater nasties, and some even climb into their mouths! By helping out someone bigger than themselves, they usually get something in return, even if it's just protection from other scary beasts.

Hermit crab

BRAIN BONUS

Who snacks on an ocean sunfish's lice?
a) great white shark
b) gulper eel
c) herring gull

Which fish makes its home in an anemone?
a) Atlantic cod
b) clownfish
c) catfish

Where is the world's largest coral reef?
a) off Australia
b) off America
c) off Argentina

(answers on page 32)

DEADLY DEFENSE

The hermit crab finds the poisonous anemone that lives on its shell so useful in keeping crab-eating predators away that it remembers its friend when it moves into a bigger house. With a perfect pincer movement, the crab gently transfers the anemone from its old shell to its new one.

CRAFTY CRAB

One crab that lives in the Indian Ocean goes the hermit crab one better. It carries around two anemones, one on the end of each front claw. If any predator dares to approach, the anemones' stinging tentacles pack a painful punch!

COCONUT CRAB

The largest land crab is the coconut crab, a relative of the hermit crab. This tropical crustacean climbs coconut trees and picks coconuts. It uses its powerful pincers to crack open the coconut and get to the tasty meat inside.

Sea anemone

VALET SERVICE

Groupers are predators that live in coral reefs. Every day or so, when they are in need of grooming, they visit a particular place on the reef to be "serviced." At the cleaning station, a troop of shrimps or tiny fish called cleaner wrasses sets to work. These creatures crawl all over the grouper, removing lice and dead skin, picking off any fungus, and even cleaning the grouper's teeth! The shrimps and cleaner fish are very hardworking, sometimes sprucing up to 50 groupers an hour. The groupers leave feeling spick-and-span—and the shrimps and wrasses have had a free meal.

Coral grouper and shrimps

STONE DEAD

The stonefish is the most poisonous fish in the sea. It looks just like a lump of rock, but it's far more deadly. If you were to accidentally tread on one, you could soon be stone dead. Spiny needles on the stonefish's fins inject a strong poison that is so painful it can make you berserk—some victims have been known to bite anyone trying to help them.

Stonefish

SANDY HIDEOUT

The stargazer gets its name from the eyes on the top of its head, but that isn't so the fish can look at the stars and dream. It's so that it can bury itself in the sand and hide, keeping an eye out for passing prey. While it waits, the stargazer remains completely still, but once a suitable meal swims past, the fish rises up as if from nowhere—and grabs it!

Stargazer

UNDERWATER SCORPION

Scorpion fish

The scorpion fish looks more like seaweed than a scorpion—and it's supposed to. Frond-like fins and wacky patterning help the fish to blend in with its background of coral-reef weeds. Its mouth is partly see-through, making it even more likely that prey will accidentally swim within striking distance and get swallowed.

HIDDEN HORROR

Lurking on the seabed are some deadly hunters.
Worst of all, their cunning camouflage makes
them invisible—until it's too late.

LEAF ME ALONE!

Some sea creatures use camouflage as defense, not to attack. The cockatoo waspfish looks just like a dead leaf, and the fish even plays dead to let the current rock it back and forth as if it were a leaf. As extra armor, the waspfish has venomous spines on its dorsal fin.

CLOWN COSTUME

The butterfly fish's coloring provides clever camouflage against the bright corals of the reef. Just right for avoiding predators—most of the time.

BRAIN BONUS

How many types of stonefish are there?

a) 1
b) 10
c) 20

How many poisonous spines does the Indian stonefish have?

a) 13—unlucky for some!
b) 7
c) 3

How long is a stargazer?

a) 4 inches
b) 20 inches
c) 39 inches

(answers on page 32)

17

DEEP WATER

Below 13,000 feet, the ocean is dark and cold. No sunlight filters down. Here in the abyss live some of the strangest-looking fish of all. Most have huge, gaping jaws and ugly, staring eyes, yet these ghoulish creatures are usually no bigger than your ruler, because food is much more scarce down there.

FEROCIOUS FANGS

The fangtooth is a deep-sea oddball with grotesque teeth. Cruising at depths of about 2,000 feet, it picks up squid and other tasty snacks. At 7,000 feet, it homes in on dragonfish and other fangy prey.

Fangtooth fish

GONE FISHING

The anglerfish lives anywhere it can find food. This underwater weirdo has to be one of the strangest fish of all. Its bulgy body doesn't need to be sleek and swift, because the best way for it to catch a meal is to keep still. Curved teeth create a cage to trap unsuspecting creatures that swim too close.

VICIOUS VIPER

At 12 inches long, the viperfish is big for a deep-sea fish. In the gloomy depths, it has come up with a clever way to attract its prey. Dangling from its dorsal fin is a glow-in-the-dark lure. This works like the worm on the end of a fishing line, but any fish that's tempted meets with the viperfish's terrifying jaws, not a juicy worm. These grip the prey with a vise-like hold.

Viperfish

FLIPPING OUT

The stomiatoid has a neat trick for gulping down a big dinner. Its whole head flips back so that it can swallow prey as wide as its own head!

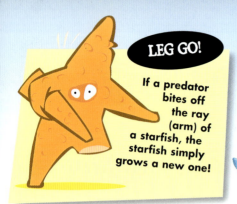

LEG GO!

If a predator bites off the ray (arm) of a starfish, the starfish simply grows a new one!

OUCH!

Lionfish

ARMY OF STINGS

The Portuguese man-of-war, a relative of the jellyfish, floats on the surface of warm seas. Its see-through body is actually a colony of small organisms called polyps. The long, trailing tentacles are covered with stinging cells called nematocysts that can deliver a nasty sting, which is strong enough to send you into shock and can affect your heartbeat or breathing.

Giant pelagic jellyfish

JELLY HEAD

In 1998, a new species of giant jellyfish was found in the eastern Pacific. Scientists named it *Chrysaora achlyos*. This rubbery monster has a 3-foot-wide purply-black bell, and its pale pink tentacles trail 20 feet behind. Scientists still haven't learned how powerful its sting is—and no one has volunteered to find out!

If you were ever stung by a jellyfish, you'd know it. All sorts of sea creatures give vicious stings, either to stun prey or to ward off an attacker. When a human being is the victim, there is usually an antidote, but sometimes the result is death.

PRICKLY PORCUPINE

The lionfish is named for its frilly mane. This is far from soft—it's made up of spines like a porcupine's quills. On the tip of each hollow spine is deadly poison, which would give a hungry shark a very nasty surprise.

SPIKES AND SPINES

Sea urchins like to be left alone to gnaw algae off the rocks or nibble on other favorite foods, such as coral. Their round bodies are covered with spines and prickles that scare away most predators. Some urchins' spines are poisonous. Divers have to be careful around urchins—not because of their poison but because puncture wounds caused by urchin prickles can easily get infected.

BRAIN BONUS

How long were the longest-ever jellyfish tentacles?

a) 34 feet
b) 57 feet
c) 120 feet

Which jellyfish's sting can kill you in minutes?

a) raspberry jellyfish
b) sea wasp
c) sea bee

How much of a jellyfish's body is made up of water?

a) 99 percent
b) 80 percent
c) 65 percent

(answers on page 32)

DEADLY POISON

Spiny pufferfish

Some creatures have developed some sharp means of defense. The pufferfish gets its name because it can puff itself up like a balloon—not that scary, until you see how it swells out its spiny, prickly skin. If a hunter is still foolish (or hungry) enough to take a bite, the puffer has a deadly weapon: poison!

DANGEROUS BEAUTY

The same poison found in the pufferfish is found in the blue-ringed octopus. This very small, very beautiful creature usually blends into the sand and rocks in the tide pool where it lives. But when it gets angry, watch out! Its skin changes to bright yellow with brilliant blue rings. It can then spit venom at its attacker.

Blue-ringed octopus

OCTOPUS NURSERY

What do you call a baby octopus? An octopod!

DISH OF DEATH

The most poisonous of all the puffers is the death puffer. Almost everything about it is horribly poisonous—its heart, liver, guts, bones, and any eggs in its stomach. Its flesh, however, is not (as long as the fish has been thoroughly cleaned). The Japanese like to gamble with death and eat the fish raw as a delicacy. This dangerous dish is known as fugu. Although chefs must train for three years before they can serve fugu, there are still accidental poisonings.

THE POISON TAKES HOLD

If you eat poisonous fugu, you'll soon know it. The first signs are a tingly mouth and dizziness. Next, you lose control of your muscles, have convulsions, and have trouble breathing. There's a 60 percent chance that you may be dead within a few hours.

DEADLY OCTOPUS

A blue-ringed octopus's bite could kill you within hours. The creature carries poison in its saliva, and if it nips you with its parrot-like beak, the poison can enter your bloodstream.

BRAIN BONUS

How many people die of fugu poisoning each year?

a) 5
b) 50
c) 100

Which of these is a Japanese "remedy" for fugu poisoning?

a) pouring boiling water down the victim's throat
b) burying the victim up to his neck in sand
c) making the victim eat shark meat

How big is a blue-ringed octopus?

a) 8 inches across
b) 20 inches across
c) 16 feet across

(answers on page 32)

DEVIL FISH

BRAIN BONUS

Why did the ancient Romans make people touch electric rays?

a) as a cure for headaches
b) as a punishment for eating meat on a fast day
c) as a punishment for forgetting their homework

How do electric rays and stingrays reproduce?

a) They attach their egg cases to strands of kelp.
b) They give birth to live young.
c) The storkray brings them.

How big is the biggest electric ray?

a) 3 feet
b) 6.5 feet
c) 10 feet

(answers on page 32)

The oceans are home to some weird creatures, and the kite-shaped ray is one of the strangest of all. Related to the sharks, there are about 400 different kinds of rays, including whip-tailed stingrays, shocking electric rays, and razor-toothed sawfish.

WHAT'S IN A NAME?

Electric rays go under many different names, but whether you call it a torpedo ray, a crampfish, or a numbfish, the hint is the same—it has the power to shock. In fact, it can send out a bolt of electricity measuring 220 volts.

HOW SHOCKING!

The electric ray gives off enough electricity to light up a lightbulb!

STING IN THE TAIL

Whether they are as small as 8 inches or as large as 6.5 feet, stingrays all have one thing in common—their whip tail. This lethal weapon, covered in poisonous spines, can be lashed so powerfully that it can get stuck in the hull of a wooden boat! Steer clear of large stingrays—a whipping from one of them can inject enough poison into your body to kill you.

Stingray

GO TO THE DEVIL

The manta ray is sometimes nicknamed "devilfish" because of the two pointy fins that look like a devil's horns sticking out of its head. This swift swimmer looks a bit like a UFO—and although it can't fly, it does sometimes heave itself out of the water and splash back down with a big belly flop!

THEY'RE ELECTRIFYING!

Electric eel

Electric rays are not alone in having the power to shock. Stargazers can do it, too, and so can some river creatures, such as the electric eel of South America and the electric catfish of Africa. The catfish's "electric" organ is a simple layer of muscle just under the skin and can send out shocks twice as strong as the electric ray's. The electric eel produces even more powerful shocks that can measure up to 650 volts—enough to kill a horse!

THAR SHE BLOWS!

Strange creatures don't have a monopoly on what's scary under the sea. Way down deep, the Earth itself does things that would fill you with terror if you could be there to see them. There are gushing vents of scalding water, flows of bubbling lava, and strange, sulfur-eating worms.

BLACK SMOKERS

Few creatures can survive where a volcanic crack on the floor of the ocean is spewing out fountains of boiling-hot water. These hot spots are called black smokers, and chimneys form around them made from the grains of minerals that shoot out from beneath the Earth's crust. One of these minerals is sulfur, which is deadly poisonous to us but makes a tasty meal for deep-water bacteria.

Giant tubeworms

BACTERIA BEANFEAST

The sulfur-rich bacteria in turn feed glowing shrimps and giant tubeworms. These stripy, red-and-white worms thrive on the stuff and grow to be as long as buses!

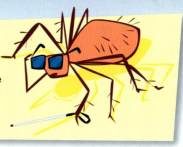
HOW LAVA-LY!

Underwater lava flow

Some underwater volcanoes ooze out lava instead of jets of hot water. The Hawaiian Islands were formed millions of years ago as lava piled up—and more islands are being born right now. In the cold ocean currents, the lava moves slowly and sets quickly, forming shapes like billowing pillows.

BIRTH OF AN ISLAND

Off the coast of Iceland in the 1960s, scientists had their first chance to witness the birth of an island when an underwater volcano erupted, spewing ash and lava above the surface of the water. The island was named Surtsey after Surtur, a fire god in Scandinavian mythology. After four years, the lava had cooled and seeds carried to the island in the seabirds' droppings took root, bringing life to the rocky surface.

BRAIN BONUS

In which year was the island of Surtsey born?

a) 1960
b) 1963
c) 1969

Where are most of the world's volcanoes?

a) on the seabed
b) in Japan
c) in California

How hot is the water that is spewed out of a black smoker?

a) 150°F
b) 330°F
c) 660°F

(answers on page 32)

CAUGHT ON FILM

Many moviemakers have tried to capture the terror of the seas on the silver screen. Some have told tales of fantastical sea beasts, while others have shown real-life horrors, such as man-eating sharks.

JAWS STORY

In the blockbuster film *Jaws* (1975), a Long Island beach resort is terrorized by a bloodthirsty great white shark. Part of the film's success was that the star of the show, the shark, was created by cleverly mixing real footage of great whites with shots of a full-size mechanical model. The movie built up to nail-biting suspense as three men headed out to sea and tried to track down the killer.

TERRIFYING TITANS

The 1981 film *Clash of the Titans* took its inspiration from Greek mythology. Its hero, Perseus, had to fight strange sea monsters on his way to rescue a beautiful princess called Andromeda. Although the movie may look dated to our eyes, at the time, moviegoers were dazzled by the film's special effects, which re-created the monsters using state-of-the-art photography and models.

A MONSTER IS BORN

The ocean is so vast that, in our imaginations at least, it could contain almost anything. All sorts of strange monsters have come out of the sea in films, but the most famous of all must be Godzilla. He has helped defend us from alien invaders, starred in his own cartoon show, and was computer-animated in 1998, when Hollywood remade the original film and set it in New York.

FEAR OF SHARKS

Jaws was the most successful horror film of all time and is the main reason why sharks have such a bad reputation today. Though sharks are predatory, shark attacks on humans are rare. Nevertheless, after seeing the film many people think twice before swimming in the ocean.

BRAIN BONUS

How much money did the *Jaws* films make?

a) $50,000
b) $5 million
c) more than $500 million

Who directed *Jaws*?

a) Steven Spielberg
b) Steven Greenburg
c) Robert White

What was Godzilla's child called?

a) Godzuki
b) King Kong
c) Repta

(answers on page 32)

UNDERWATER ODYSSEY

In the film *20,000 Leagues Under the Sea,* Captain Nemo uses his fish-shaped submarine, the *Nautilus,* to sink warships. How far did he travel? Twenty thousand leagues, or almost 70,000 miles.

29

SINGING SIRENS

Stories about mermaids have been around for over 5,000 years and are found in Hindu legends as well as European folklore. Half woman, half fish, mermaids are often blamed for luring sailors to their deaths on the rocks by charming them with their sweet, soulful songs. Countless mermaid movies have been made, usually focusing on the hopeless love between a human man and a mermaid.

Giant squid

MERMAID DISPLAYS

In the 1500s, showmen traveled from town to town offering a bizarre attraction: real mermaids! By the 1800s, mermaids were a craze. Some of the specimens were fakes, others were dried-up jenny hanivers, a tropical fish that was modified to look more or less human.

STRETCHY SQUID

Is the giant squid a real-life kraken? This monstrous mollusk is as long as three tractor-trailers!

SAILORS' STORIES

Long before movies, storytellers spun fantastical tales of the sea. Sailors came home with crazy stories of sea dragons, serpents, and humanlike creatures, while back in ancient times, writers recorded myths of epic sea journeys featuring magical monsters.

THE KRAKEN AWAKES

The mythical kraken, with its long, squirming tentacles, appears in Scandinavian legends. This sea dragon may have been inspired by sightings of a real giant squid.

SCYLLA'S HEADS

Greek myths are big on monsters, and Scylla must be one of the scariest. Scylla was the sea monster that the Greek hero Odysseus had to get past on his epic journey. Scylla had six heads, twelve feet, and a triple row of gnashing teeth! Scylla began life as a beautiful maiden but was turned into a monster by a jealous sorceress named Circe.

BRAIN BONUS

What kind of creature was Sebastian in *The Little Mermaid*?

a) a crab
b) a seagull
c) an octopus

How many of Odysseus' men did Scylla devour?

a) none
b) six
c) 100

Which creature was once mistaken for a mermaid?

a) a manta ray
b) a catfish
c) a manatee

(answers on page 32)

BRAIN BONUS ANSWERS

p. 3   **c)** 25. **b)** 35 mph. **c)** 172–252. Compare that to the bottlenose dolphin, which has only 76–98 teeth.

p. 5   **a) b) c)** All three fishes are sharks. **b)** a month or two. Sharks have rows and rows of sharp teeth. When a tooth is lost, a new tooth fills in from behind. **c)** six times. Tiger sharks can swim over 20 mph.

p. 7   **b)** more than 3 feet. **b)** From 30 to 100 people are bitten by sharks while only from 2 to 15 people are killed by sharks each year. **a)** Only 32 of the 350 species of shark have attacked humans. These sharks have three things in common: they eat fish or marine mammals, they are large, and they hunt in warm water near the coasts where humans like to swim.

p. 8   **a)** 4 feet. **b)** tailor. **b)** two.

p. 10   **c)** 59 feet. **c)** The longest blue whale ever recorded was 110 feet long and weighed 380,000 pounds—as much as 1,500 professional football players. **a)** The basking shark, nearly 40 feet long, feeds on plankton and krill that it filters from huge gulps of seawater.

p. 13   **a)** The saltwater crocodile lives in the ocean near the coast of India, southern China, and Malaysia. It can grow up to 30 feet long, making it one of the largest living reptiles in the world. **b)** Since a sea snake must drink saltwater, a gland near its tongue gets rid of the excess salt it has swallowed. **c)** oarfish.

p. 14   **c)** herring gull. **b)** The clownfish lives among the anemone's stinging tentacles, which protect the clownfish from predators. In return, the clownfish eats any debris that floats into the anemone. **a)** Off Australia is the world's largest coral reef, the Great Barrier Reef, which is over 1,200 miles long.

p. 17   **c)** 20. **a)** 13. **a)** 4 inches.

p. 18   **c)** 100. **a)** scales. **a)** 2 inches.

p. 21   **c)** 120 feet. **b)** The sea wasp jellyfish, with deadly stinging cells on each of its 60 tentacles, has enough venom to kill several humans. **a)** 99 percent.

p. 23   **b)** 50. **b)** burying the victim up to his neck in sand. **a)** 8 inches across.

p. 24   **a)** as a cure for headaches. **b)** They give birth to live young. **b)** 6.5 feet long.

p. 27   **b)** 1963. **a)** on the seabed. **c)** 660° F.

p. 29   **c)** more than $500 million. **a)** Steven Spielberg. **a)** Godzuki.

p. 31   **a)** a crab. **b)** six. **c)** Manatees, or sea cows, are large marine mammals that early sailors often mistook for mermaids.